INSIDE THE
NFL

WASHINGTON
REDSKINS

BY TONY HUNTER

SportsZone

An Imprint of Abdo Publishing
abdobooks.com

abdobooks.com

Published by Abdo Publishing, a division of ABDO, PO Box 398166, Minneapolis, Minnesota 55439. Copyright © 2020 by Abdo Consulting Group, Inc. International copyrights reserved in all countries. No part of this book may be reproduced in any form without written permission from the publisher. SportsZone™ is a trademark and logo of Abdo Publishing.

Printed in the United States of America, North Mankato, Minnesota
042019
092019

Cover Photo: Andrew Harnik/AP Images
Interior Photos: Ronald C. Modra/Sports Illustrated/Set Number: X27986/Getty Images, 4–5; Al Messerschmidt/AP Images, 7; AP Images, 9, 10–11, 15, 17, 22, 29, 43; NFL Photos/ AP Images, 19, 34; Harvey Georges/AP Images, 21; Arnie Sachs/picture-alliance/dpa/ AP Images, 25; Mark Duncan/AP Images, 27; John Biever/Sports Illustrated/Set Number: X36039 TK2 R5 F16/AP Images, 31; Elise Amendola/AP Images, 32; Al Tielemans/Sports Illustrated/SetNumber: X78696 TK1 R2 F110/AP Images, 36–37; Nick Wass/AP Images, 39; Richard Lipski/AP Images, 40

Editor: Patrick Donnelly
Series Designer: Craig Hinton

Library of Congress Control Number: 2018966048

Publisher's Cataloging-in-Publication Data

Names: Hunter, Tony, author.
Title: Washington Redskins / by Tony Hunter
Description: Minneapolis, Minnesota: Abdo Publishing, 2020 | Series: Inside the NFL | Includes online resources and index.
Identifiers: ISBN 9781532118678 (lib. bdg.) | ISBN 9781532172854 (ebook)
Subjects: LCSH: Washington Redskins (Football team)--Juvenile literature. | National Football League--Juvenile literature. | Football teams--Juvenile literature. | American football-- Juvenile literature.
Classification: DDC 796.33264--dc23

TABLE OF
CONTENTS

CHAPTER 1

RETURN
TO GLORY

Joe Gibbs had a tough decision to make. The Washington Redskins faced a fourth down at the Miami Dolphins' 43-yard line. It was early in the fourth quarter of Super Bowl XVII at the Rose Bowl in Pasadena, California, on January 30, 1983. Washington trailed 17–13. The Redskins needed less than a yard for the first down.

A punt could have pinned Miami deep in its own territory. But Gibbs, Washington's head coach, decided to go for the first down. The Redskins called "70 chip." It was designed for running back John Riggins to take the handoff and run left. It would go down as one of the most dramatic plays in team history.

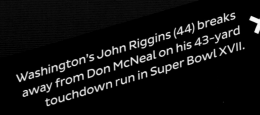

Washington's John Riggins (44) breaks away from Don McNeal on his 43-yard touchdown run in Super Bowl XVII.

JOE GIBBS

Joe Gibbs coached the Redskins from 1981 to 1992 and again from 2004 to 2007. During his first stint, Gibbs guided Washington to three Super Bowls, four NFC titles, five NFC East titles, and eight playoff berths. He led the Redskins to two playoff berths in his second stint.

Gibbs retired in 1993 to pursue another competitive passion—running a NASCAR team. But he returned to the Redskins in 2004. He retired again after the 2007 season, at age 67.

Gibbs was completing his second season as Redskins coach. He would go on to win three Super Bowls with Washington and lead the Redskins to a fourth during his first stint as the team's coach, from 1981 to 1992.

But as of January 1983, the Redskins had not yet won a Super Bowl. In fact, Washington had not won a National Football League (NFL) title since 1942, 24 years before the first Super Bowl. The team's fans were desperate for one. The 1982 season was Washington's best in a decade. The Redskins went 8–1 in a strike-shortened year. They then won three straight National Football Conference (NFC) playoff games to get to Super Bowl XVII.

Washington fell behind Miami early. The Dolphins were led by a great defense and coach Don Shula. He had already won two Super Bowls and was coaching in his fifth. It appeared that the veteran Shula might have an edge on the inexperienced Gibbs.

✗ Redskins quarterback Joe Theismann scrambles out of the pocket during Super Bowl XVII.

Only 10 minutes remained in the game as Washington faced the key fourth-down play. Quarterback Joe Theismann took the snap and handed the ball to Riggins, who ran left. Cornerback Don McNeal closed in quickly at the line of scrimmage. He was unblocked and had a free shot at Riggins. He hit the ball carrier around the waist before the first-down marker.

But few cornerbacks could bring down the 6-foot-2, 240-pound Riggins. He continued churning his feet as McNeal hit him. The cornerback then slid down Riggins's legs and fell to the ground. Riggins accelerated past the first-down marker,

JOHN RIGGINS

John Riggins played running back for the Redskins from 1976 to 1979 and 1981 to 1985. He sat out the 1980 season because of a contract dispute. Riggins rushed for 166 yards and a touchdown in the Super Bowl XVII win. The 166 yards were a Super Bowl record at the time. Through 2018 Riggins was the Redskins' all-time leading rusher with 7,472 yards. Nicknamed "The Diesel," he was inducted into the Pro Football Hall of Fame in 1992. Riggins was known as a workhorse back who gained the tough yards inside and near the goal line. He scored 128 career touchdowns, including postseason games; 59 of them were on 1-yard runs.

leaving McNeal behind. No other Miami players stood in his way. Not only would Riggins get the first down—he was going to score.

As Riggins raced down the sideline into the end zone, anyone listening to the Redskins' radio broadcast heard the call by play-by-play man Frank Herzog: "He's gone! He's gone! Touchdown, Washington Redskins!"

Washington had the lead for the first time in the game. The Redskins' defense then stuffed the Dolphins, and the offense embarked on another big drive. When Theismann tossed a 6-yard touchdown pass to wide receiver Charlie Brown with just under two minutes to play, Washington went ahead 27–17. That would be the final score.

As Theismann walked off the field, he held the ball high with one hand. With his other hand, he stuck his index finger

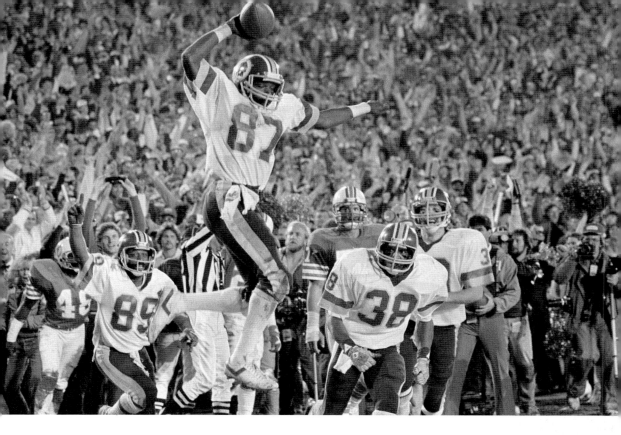

✗ Washington wide receiver Charlie Brown (87) celebrates his touchdown that sealed the Super Bowl victory for the Redskins.

in the air: The Redskins were number one. Riggins was named the game's Most Valuable Player (MVP). "Ron [Reagan] may be president," Riggins said, "but tonight I'm king."

Washington finally had its first Super Bowl win and its first NFL title in four decades. Just as important, a new dynasty was born. The Redskins were back on top—where fans believed the team belonged. After all, the Redskins had been one of the NFL's best teams when they started playing in Washington nearly a half century earlier.

CHAPTER 2

THE BIRTH OF A TRADITION

George Preston Marshall was a successful businessman in Washington, DC, in the early 1930s. He wanted to own a professional sports team. In 1932 the NFL wanted to add a team in Boston. Marshall was offered a chance to buy a franchise and place it in Boston. It would be one of only eight teams in the NFL, which began in 1920.

Marshall leapt at the opportunity. The Boston Braves went 4–4–2 in their opening season in the NFL. The next year, the team moved to Fenway Park and Marshall changed its nickname to the Redskins. The Boston Redskins soon became one of the NFL's top squads. They reached the championship game in 1936, falling to the Green Bay Packers.

Quarterback Sammy Baugh joined the Redskins in 1937, the year they moved to Washington, DC, and won an NFL title.

CONTROVERSIAL NAME

The name "Redskins" is a derogatory term used to refer to Native Americans. The origin of its use as a team nickname is the subject of some dispute. Some reports say that George Preston Marshall changed the name from Braves to Redskins because the team was moving from the Boston Braves' park to the home of the Boston Red Sox. Other stories say the name honors a former coach who was thought to be of Native American ancestry.

The name has triggered numerous protests and campaigns trying to convince current owner Daniel Snyder to change it. But Snyder refuses. He says he believes the name is important to the history of the team and the success it has had.

Still, some journalists have decided they aren't comfortable using the team's nickname when reporting football news. Some newspapers and individual media members have begun refusing to use the term, instead referring to the Redskins as the "Washington football team."

After that season, Marshall made another change. The Redskins had experienced poor attendance for much of their five years in Boston. Marshall was losing thousands of dollars. So he announced that he was moving the team. It would play in Marshall's adopted hometown of Washington, DC.

With that, the Washington Redskins were born. The decision to move paid off. The Redskins' first decade in Washington was their first golden era. From 1937 to 1945, the team won two NFL crowns, played in five title games, and went 70–27–5, including playoff games.

The Redskins had one of the NFL's best players in Sammy Baugh. In that era, most players stayed on the field for offense and defense, and some even kicked and punted, too. Baugh stood out at quarterback, defensive back, and punter.

Baugh led the Redskins to a 7–3 start in 1937, their first season in Washington. The squad drew more than 20,000 fans in three of its six home games, a good number in the NFL at the time. The Redskins' final regular-season game came on the road against the New York Giants. The winner would capture the Eastern Division crown and play for the NFL title.

Washington crushed New York 49–14. A week later, the Redskins faced the Chicago Bears in the NFL Championship Game, held at Chicago's Wrigley Field. Baugh threw for 335 yards and three touchdowns as Washington won 28–21 for the team's first NFL title.

The Redskins advanced to the NFL Championship Game again after the 1940 season. But this time the Bears routed them. Washington fell 73–0 to visiting Chicago. The Bears had 519 yards of offense, including 381 rushing. They intercepted eight passes, returning three for touchdowns.

COMPLICATED LEGACY

George Preston Marshall was the Redskins' first owner, from 1932 until his death in 1969. He helped found the team in Boston, then moved it to Washington, DC, in 1937. Marshall launched a radio network that broadcast Redskins games throughout the southern United States. That created a base of Redskins fans miles from Washington. He was inducted into the Pro Football Hall of Fame in 1963.

Marshall's legacy remains complicated, however. His team was the last to integrate its roster. Beginning in 1934, league owners refused to sign black players. Marshall rallied his fellow owners to maintain that policy, but eventually his efforts proved unsuccessful.

The Los Angeles Rams reintegrated the league by signing running back Kenny Washington in 1946. Soon the Redskins were the final team with an all-white roster. In 1961 the US government threatened to revoke the lease it granted Marshall for a new stadium built on government-owned property if he refused to integrate his team. NFL Commissioner Pete Rozelle intervened and eventually convinced Marshall to give in. The first black player to take the field for the Redskins was wide receiver Bobby Mitchell in 1962.

In 1942 the Redskins got their revenge on the Bears. Washington went 10–1 and won the Eastern Division. The team's opponent in the title game again was the Bears. Chicago had won 18 straight games, including the 1941 title. Baugh threw the go-ahead touchdown pass as the Redskins won 14–6. The fans at Washington's Griffith Stadium were thrilled.

✗ The Redskins' Sammy Baugh looks to pass against the Bears in the 1942 NFL Championship Game. Washington won 14–6.

Washington won the division again in 1943 and 1945. The Bears beat the Redskins 41–21 to win the 1943 title, and the Cleveland Rams edged them 15–14 in the 1945 championship game.

Nevertheless, the Redskins were one of the NFL's best teams. They were confident that they would have other shots to win another league championship soon. But the franchise had to wait a long time before fielding another winning team.

CHAPTER 3

FROM BOTTOM TO TOP

After being one of the NFL's dominant teams for a decade, the Redskins failed to reach the postseason from 1946 to 1970. Washington struggled for several reasons. The franchise made bad decisions, trading away future stars such as quarterback Charlie Conerly and safety Paul Krause. In addition, the Redskins refused to build their roster to its full potential by signing talented black players, instead remaining an all-white team until 1962.

Nobody expected such a slide after 1945. The Redskins had just played in the NFL Championship Game for the sixth time in 10 seasons. But before the next season, owner George Preston Marshall fired head coach Dud DeGroot.

Bobby Mitchell makes a catch over the Cardinals' Norman Beal in 1962.

BOBBY MITCHELL

Bobby Mitchell starred for the Redskins from 1962 to 1968. He played running back for the Cleveland Browns from 1958 to 1961. Washington converted him to wide receiver.

Mitchell was the first black player to join the Redskins and succeeded despite the franchise's checkered past regarding race relations. "Bobby laid a lot of foundation," said Brig Owens, a Redskins safety from 1966 to 1977. "It took a special person to come here [as the first African-American player]. Every time they put Bobby in a position to fail, he succeeded, not just in a small way, but in a major way."

Mitchell was named to the Pro Bowl four times over his career. He racked up 521 career receptions and 91 touchdowns overall. When he retired in 1968, he ranked fifth all-time in touchdowns in the NFL.

Turk Edwards took over as head coach. He led Washington to a 16–18–1 mark in three seasons.

After three straight losing seasons, Marshall let Edwards go and hired Curly Lambeau in 1952. Lambeau had guided the Green Bay Packers to six NFL titles. Not even Lambeau could help the Redskins, though. They went a combined 10–13–1 in two seasons before Marshall fired him.

The Redskins traded for Bobby Mitchell before the 1962 season. Mitchell was a star running back with the Cleveland

Redskins quarterback Sonny Jurgensen walks off the field in 1967. Washington had plenty of talent in the 1950s and the 1960s but struggled as a team.

Browns. He quickly made the Redskins better. He had 72 catches for 1,384 yards in the 1962 season.

After a losing season in 1963, the Redskins were aggressive in the offseason. They traded for two stars—quarterback Sonny Jurgensen and linebacker Sam Huff. They also drafted wide receiver Charley Taylor. All three would eventually be inducted into the Pro Football Hall of Fame. Yet over the next five years, the best record the Redskins could manage was 7–7 in 1966.

Throughout much of the 1960s, the Redskins had a talented offense that included Mitchell, Jurgensen, Taylor, and tight end Jerry Smith. Washington's defense in the 1960s, however, was terrible.

By the late 1960s, Marshall was ailing. Edward Bennett Williams became the Redskins' owner. In 1969 Williams outbid a few other teams to hire Vince Lombardi. Lombardi had coached the Packers to five NFL titles in the 1960s, including wins in the first two Super Bowls after the 1966 and 1967 seasons. He had retired to become Green Bay's general manager in 1968. But he missed coaching.

Lombardi turned around the Redskins quickly. They started the 1969 season 4–1–1. But a late-season loss to the Los Angeles Rams helped give the Dallas Cowboys the division title and kept the Redskins out of the playoffs. Washington finished 7–5–2 and was optimistic about its chances in 1970.

Then tragedy struck. During the offseason, Lombardi was diagnosed with cancer. He died during training camp.

✕ The Redskins hired legendary coach Vince Lombardi in 1969. He led the team to a winning season that year.

Offensive line coach Bill Austin served as interim head coach. But the Redskins stumbled to a 6–8 record that year.

It seemed that no matter what the Redskins did, they could not become consistent winners. After the 1970 season, Williams fired Austin. Just as he did when he hired Lombardi, he turned to another veteran coach: George Allen.

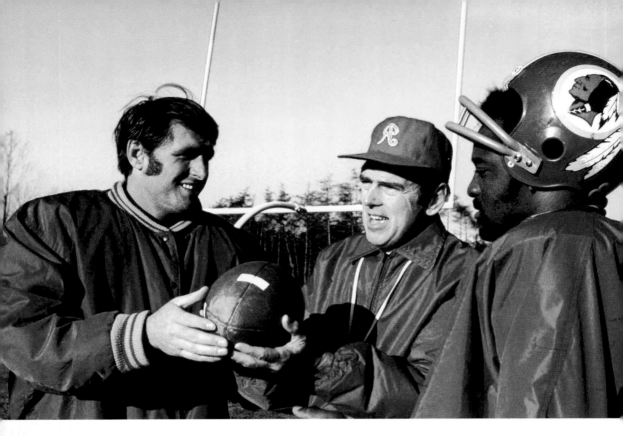

✕ Head coach George Allen, *center*, talks strategy with quarterback Billy Kilmer, *left*, and running back Larry Brown.

Allen had coached the Los Angeles Rams from 1966 to 1970. Williams, the Redskins' owner, then hired Allen as coach and general manager in 1971. Allen made big changes. He traded for several former Rams, including defensive end Diron Talbert and linebacker Jack Pardee. Allen also went with veteran Billy Kilmer as his quarterback over Jurgensen.

Washington finished in second place in the NFC East in 1971. But the Redskins earned the NFC's lone wild-card berth. They lost their playoff opener 24–20 to the 49ers at

San Francisco. Yet they had enjoyed a successful season. They had finally become winners again.

The Redskins had big expectations heading into 1972. Those expectations were met. The 11–3 Redskins won the NFC East title. Running back Larry Brown was named the NFL's MVP.

Washington defeated Green Bay 16–3 in the divisional round of the playoffs to set up an NFC Championship Game matchup with the Dallas Cowboys. It was not close. Kilmer completed 14 of 18 passes, including two touchdown passes to Taylor. The Redskins held the defending Super Bowl champion Cowboys to 169 yards in a 26–3 blowout. The win put them in their first Super Bowl.

The Redskins still had to play the Super Bowl, though. Two weeks later, they lost Super Bowl VII to the undefeated Miami

GEORGE ALLEN

George Allen coached the Redskins from 1971 to 1977. He was also the team's general manager and led them to an NFC title and five playoff berths.

He was twice named NFL Coach of the Year—in 1967 with the Los Angeles Rams, and again in 1971 in his first year with Washington.

A native of Michigan, Allen was inducted into the Pro Football Hall of Fame in 2002. He was known as an innovator. Allen was the first head coach to employ a special teams coach. He also pioneered the nickel defense, using an extra defensive back on passing downs.

Dolphins 14–7 at Los Angeles Memorial Coliseum. Kilmer threw three interceptions. The Redskins managed just 228 yards. The Dolphins became the first team to finish a season without a loss at 17–0.

Despite the loss to the Dolphins, the Redskins expected to be back in the Super Bowl. Washington qualified for the playoffs again in 1973, 1974, and 1976. The Redskins went 10–4 each of those seasons. They tied for the division title twice. But there would be no more Super Bowls for Washington in the 1970s.

After the 1977 season, Allen and Williams could not agree on a new contract. Williams fired Allen and replaced him as coach with Pardee. He had been the Chicago Bears' head coach the previous three seasons. Washington started 6–0 in 1978 but finished 8–8.

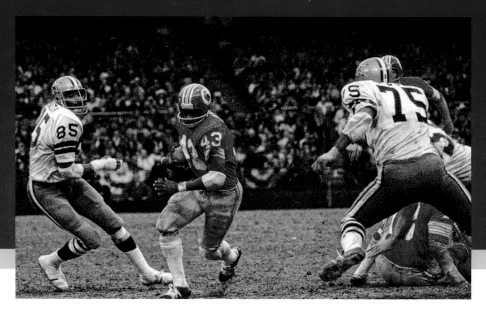

Larry Brown bursts through a hole in Washington's 1972 NFC Championship Game victory over Dallas.

The Redskins went 10–6 in 1979. But the Bears, who had the same record, earned the final NFC wild-card berth on a tiebreaker. Washington fell apart in 1980. Running back John Riggins sat out the season in a contract dispute. Washington finished 6–10, and Pardee was fired.

The future would bring a lot of changes. Many of the players were getting old and would have to be replaced. Williams stepped down. Jack Kent Cooke replaced him as the primary owner. Cooke and general manager Bobby Beathard chose little-known San Diego Chargers offensive coordinator Joe Gibbs as the next coach. Finally, the Redskins had found the man to lead them back to the top.

CHAPTER 4

DYNASTY

Mark Rypien dropped back, looked to his right, and lofted a pass toward the sideline. The ball fell into the hands of wide receiver Gary Clark. Clark ran into the end zone, extending Washington's lead in Super Bowl XXVI to 20 points over the Buffalo Bills. The Redskins would win 37–24 on January 26, 1992, at the Metrodome in Minneapolis.

The victory gave Washington its third Super Bowl title in 10 seasons. It was the exclamation point on an NFL dynasty.

The two main keys to the Redskins' success were excellent coaching and chemistry. "We didn't have a lot of talent, but we all knew what we had to do to win: play well together," said Art Monk, a Redskins wide receiver from 1980 to 1993.

The golden era did not start so well. Joe Gibbs lost his first five games as Redskins coach in 1981. Gibbs and

Quarterback Mark Rypien celebrates a Washington touchdown against Buffalo in Super Bowl XXVI.

JOE THEISMANN

The Miami Dolphins drafted Joe Theismann out of Notre Dame in 1971, but he signed with the Canadian Football League's Toronto Argonauts. Washington traded for the rights to sign him in 1974, and he spent his first NFL season with the Redskins as their punt returner. He took over as the team's starting quarterback in 1978 and held the job until 1985. Theismann led the 1982 Redskins to the NFL title. He retired with 25,206 career passing yards, still the most in team history through 2018. Theismann was named the NFL's MVP in 1983, when he threw for 3,714 yards and 29 touchdowns.

quarterback Joe Theismann settled some communication problems and Washington rebounded to finish with an 8–8 record.

Washington went 8–1 in the 1982 season, which was shortened because of a players' strike. The top-seeded Redskins beat the Detroit Lions 31–7 and the Minnesota Vikings 21–7 in the playoffs to reach the NFC Championship Game. John Riggins ran for two touchdowns and defensive tackle Darryl Grant returned an interception 10 yards for a score as Washington beat the rival Dallas Cowboys 31–17. Fans at RFK Stadium stormed the field and ripped down the goalposts.

Washington then beat the Miami Dolphins in Super Bowl XVII for its first NFL title in 40 years. Riggins provided the memorable 43-yard touchdown run in the fourth quarter.

✕ John Riggins dives for a 1-yard touchdown in the Redskins' 31–17 NFC Championship Game win over the Cowboys on January 22, 1983.

The Redskins went 14–2 the next season and earned the NFC's No. 1 seed again. Washington edged the San Francisco 49ers 24–21 in the NFC Championship Game. The Redskins fell short of a second straight Super Bowl title two weeks later. They lost Super Bowl XVIII to the Los Angeles Raiders 38–9. Although they had set an NFL record in the regular season

DARRELL GREEN

Darrell Green played cornerback for the Redskins from 1983 to 2002. He set an NFL record with an interception in 19 straight seasons. Green was named an All-Pro four times. He was inducted into the Pro Football Hall of Fame in 2008. Green was short for his position (5 feet 9 inches) but extremely fast. He became a cornerback who could shut down opposing receivers by also using toughness.

with 541 points, the Redskins' high-powered offense could not get anything going against the Raiders.

The Redskins captured another NFC East title in 1984. But Washington lost to the Chicago Bears in the divisional round of the playoffs. The Redskins then failed to reach the postseason in 1985 despite tying for the best record in the NFC East at 10–6.

Heading into 1986, the Redskins had to reload after Theismann and Riggins retired. Quarterback Jay Schroeder, running back George Rogers, and Clark led Washington's offense that season. The team finished 12–4. The Redskins beat the visiting Rams in a wild-card playoff game and then traveled to Chicago. The 14–2 Bears were the defending Super Bowl champions. But Washington held star running back Walter Payton to 38 rushing yards and won 27–13. The next week, the visiting Redskins lost 17–0 to the eventual Super Bowl–champion New York Giants in the NFC Championship Game.

✕ Darrell Green was a fixture with the Redskins for 20 seasons.

Washington finished 11–4 in a strike-shortened 1987 season and won the division. In the regular-season finale, backup Doug Williams replaced an ineffective Schroeder to rally the Redskins past the host Vikings. Gibbs announced that Williams would start in the playoffs.

The Redskins edged the host Bears 21–17 in the divisional round and held off the visiting Vikings 17–10 in the NFC Championship Game. Cornerback Darrell Green hit Minnesota running back Darrin Nelson near the goal line in the closing seconds to break up a fourth-down pass.

✕ Doug Williams passed for 340 yards in Washington's 42–10 rout of Denver in Super Bowl XXII on January 31, 1988.

Super Bowl XXII two weeks later in San Diego was no contest. The Denver Broncos, led by star quarterback John Elway, were favored to win, and they even took a 10–0 lead after the first quarter. But the Redskins scored 35 points in the second quarter, a Super Bowl record. Washington won 42–10. Two Redskins players set Super Bowl records that day: running back Timmy Smith rushed for 204 yards, and wide receiver Ricky Sanders posted 193 receiving yards. Williams threw four touchdown passes and was named the game's MVP. He became the first black quarterback to start for a Super Bowl champion.

"In that Super Bowl, it took us a quarter to settle down, but once we did, nobody was going to beat us that day," Clark said.

The Redskins went 7–9 in 1988 and 10–6 in 1989 and did not make the playoffs either season. In 1990 the Redskins relied on running back Earnest Byner down the stretch to finish 10–6 and make the postseason. Washington beat host Philadelphia 20–6 in a wild-card game. The Redskins then lost at San Francisco in the divisional round. But Washington had returned to its roots under Gibbs: a dominant running game that opened up space for the passing game.

That is exactly how the 1991 season played out. Byner (1,048 yards), rookie Ricky Ervins (680 yards), and fullback Gerald Riggs (11 touchdowns) dominated on the ground. Rypien threw for more than 3,500 yards and 28 touchdowns.

Washington went 14–2, then cruised through the NFC playoffs with victories over the Atlanta Falcons and the Detroit Lions. In Super Bowl XXVI, Buffalo was no match for the Redskins on either side of the ball. Rypien, who threw for two

✗ Wide receiver Gary Clark runs with the ball after making a catch in the Redskins' 37–24 win over the Bills in Super Bowl XXVI.

touchdowns and 292 yards, was named the game's MVP. Riggs

added two touchdowns. The defense forced five turnovers.

"The Redskins had one of those teams," Bills quarterback Jim Kelly said. "You almost had to play a perfect game to beat them."

The Super Bowl XXVI win is remembered as the unofficial end of an era. The Redskins were aging, and Gibbs was tiring. In 1992, Washington finished 9–7, beat Minnesota in a wild-card game, and then lost to San Francisco in the divisional round.

A few months later, Gibbs retired. Defensive coordinator Richie Petitbon replaced Gibbs. Unfortunately for Washington, it marked the beginning of an era in which the team would struggle.

THE HOGS

"The Hogs" was the colorful nickname for the Redskins' big, strong offensive linemen and tight ends. They dominated opposing defenses in the 1980s and the 1990s and formed the foundation for the three NFL championship teams.

Tackles Joe Jacoby and George Starke, guards Russ Grimm and Mark May, center Jeff Bostic, and tight ends Rick Walker and Don Warren were the original Hogs. Tackles Jim Lachey and Ed Simmons and guards Raleigh McKenzie and Mark Schlereth later became Hogs as well. The nickname came from offensive line coach Joe Bugel during training camp in 1982.

CHAPTER 5

FRUSTRATION

The Redskins' run of success from the 1981 through 1992 seasons was enjoyable for the team and its fans. But the next era of Redskins football was particularly agonizing.

After coach Joe Gibbs retired, the Redskins fell apart. The team went 4–12 in 1993. Richie Petitbon was fired as coach after the season and replaced by Norv Turner, a former Dallas assistant. Washington went a combined 9–23 in its first two seasons under Turner.

The Redskins finished 9–7 in 1996 and 8–7–1 in 1997 but missed the playoffs both times. When Washington went 6–10 in 1998, many people thought that the team would fire Turner. Owner Jack Kent Cooke had died in 1997. Daniel Snyder bought the team. But the sale was not completed until July 1999. By then it was too late to replace Turner.

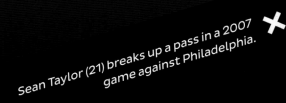

Sean Taylor (21) breaks up a pass in a 2007 game against Philadelphia.

The Redskins, led by newly acquired quarterback Brad Johnson, finished 10–6 in 1999. They won the NFC East title. Washington beat the visiting Detroit Lions 27–13 in the first round of the playoffs but then fell 14–13 to host Tampa Bay.

The 2000 offseason marked the real beginning of the Daniel Snyder era. Instead of allowing a true football expert to run the team, the young owner made many of the moves himself.

Washington began the 2000 season 6–2 but finished 8–8 and missed the playoffs. Snyder fired Turner with three games left. Coaches Marty Schottenheimer (8–8 in 2001) and Steve Spurrier (12–20 from 2002 to 2003) were given shots to turn the team around but could not do it.

Snyder shocked nearly everyone with his next coaching hire. After 11 years away, Gibbs returned to his role as head coach. The rebuilding Redskins went 6–10 in 2004. But they finished 10–6 in 2005 and qualified for the postseason. Running back Clinton Portis and wide receiver Santana Moss led the way. The Redskins beat the host Buccaneers 17–10 in the wild-card round. Washington then lost 20–10 at Seattle.

The Redskins slumped to 5–11 in 2006. Washington was 5–3 at the halfway point of the 2007 season when tragedy struck the team again. Star safety Sean Taylor was injured in a loss

Team owner Daniel Snyder, *left*, confers with head coach Mike Shanahan at a 2010 practice.

to the Philadelphia Eagles. While he was recovering at home in Florida, burglars broke into his house and shot him. Taylor died the next day, on November 27. The Redskins were crushed. They lost their next game, to the Buffalo Bills, to fall to 5–7.

Washington rallied to earn a wild-card berth. But the team ran out of gas in the first round, falling 35–14 at Seattle. The next week, Gibbs said he was retiring for good.

Snyder brought in Jim Zorn as head coach. His two seasons were a disaster. Washington finished in last place in the NFC East and Zorn was let go in 2009. Mike Shanahan took over for Zorn. He came in with a strong pedigree after

Robert Griffin III was a dual-threat quarterback who led the Redskins to the playoffs in his rookie season.

winning a pair of Super Bowls with the Denver Broncos. He made a significant change when he helped the team bring in quarterback Donovan McNabb, who had been a pain in the side of Washington for years as he led the division-rival Eagles.

McNabb lasted just one season as the Redskins quarterback as they finished 6–10. In 2011 the team struggled once again with mediocre quarterback play. In 2012 Washington knew it needed a big-time quarterback.

The Redskins responded by acquiring the No. 2 overall pick in the 2012 NFL Draft. They used it to select Robert Griffin III. He was a mobile quarterback who excited fans with his speed.

Griffin's rookie season was a success. In the first quarter of his first game, Griffin excited fans with an 88-yard touchdown pass to Pierre Garcon as the Redskins won at New Orleans.

Washington won the NFC East with a 10–6 record. However, Griffin suffered a serious knee injury as the Redskins lost to the Seahawks in the playoffs. Washington never got back to prominence with Griffin as quarterback.

The next season, Griffin returned but struggled to stay healthy as Washington went 3–13. Shanahan was replaced by Jay Gruden. He turned to another quarterback who was taken by the Redskins in the 2012 Draft. Selected in the fourth round, Kirk Cousins was expected to be a backup. But Cousins didn't play much like a backup. By 2015 he had the Redskins back in the playoffs. Cousins helped the Redskins score the 10th-most points in the NFL during that season.

Cousins continued to lead Washington but did not make the playoffs in 2016 or 2017. The Redskins decided they did not want to give Cousins a long-term contract and let him become a free agent. They traded for quarterback Alex Smith in 2018, but Smith suffered a season-ending leg injury in Week 11. It was back to the drawing board for the Redskins as they searched for their next franchise quarterback.

TIMELINE

The Redskins are born as the Boston Braves.

1932

The host Braves defeat the New York Giants 14–6 on October 9 for their first win in franchise history.

1932

The club, now called the Redskins, moves to Washington. The Redskins defeat the host Chicago Bears 28–21 on December 12 to win their first NFL title.

1937

The Redskins beat the visiting Bears 14–6 on December 13 to win another NFL title.

1942

Bobby Mitchell becomes the first black player to play for the Redskins after he is traded by the Cleveland Browns to Washington.

1962

The Redskins hire legendary former Green Bay Packers coach Vince Lombardi as their new head coach.

1969

Former Los Angeles Rams head coach George Allen takes over in the same role in Washington.

1971

The Redskins crush the rival Dallas Cowboys 26–3 on December 31 in the NFC Championship Game at RFK Stadium, clinching their first Super Bowl berth.

1972

The unbeaten Miami Dolphins defeat the Redskins 14–7 on January 14 in Super Bowl VII.

1973

Washington hires Joe Gibbs as its new head coach.

1981

The Redskins defeat the Dolphins 27–17 on January 30 in Super Bowl XVII, winning their first NFL title since 1942.

1983

Washington loses 38–9 to the Los Angeles Raiders on January 22 in Super Bowl XVIII.

1984

The Redskins blast the Denver Broncos 42–10 in Super Bowl XXII on January 31.

1988

On January 26, Washington tops the Buffalo Bills 37–24 in the Super Bowl, winning a third NFL title in 10 seasons.

1992

Gibbs retires as coach on March 5, citing fatigue.

1993

Gibbs returns as head coach 11 years after he retired.

2004

Washington beats visiting Dallas 27–6 on December 30. The win was the Redskins' fourth straight and secured a playoff spot.

2007

The Redskins trade up in the NFL Draft to select quarterback Robert Griffin III with the No. 2 pick.

2012

Jay Gruden is hired as head coach and becomes the eighth to serve in that role since Daniel Snyder took over as owner in 1999.

2014

The Redskins waste a hot start, going 1–6 down the stretch to miss the playoffs for the third straight season.

2018

QUICK STATS

FRANCHISE HISTORY

Boston Braves (1932)
Boston Redskins (1933–36)
Washington Redskins (1937–)

SUPER BOWLS
(wins in bold)

1972 (VII), **1982 (XVII)**, 1983 (XVIII),
1987 (XXII), **1991 (XXVI)**

NFL CHAMPIONSHIP GAMES
(1933–69, wins in bold)

1936, **1937**, 1940, **1942**, 1943, 1945

NFC CHAMPIONSHIP GAMES
(since 1970 AFL-NFL merger)

1972, 1982, 1983, 1986, 1987, 1991

KEY COACHES

George Allen (1971–77):
  67–30–1, 2–5 (playoffs)
Joe Gibbs (1981–92, 2004–07):
  154–94, 17–7 (playoffs)

KEY PLAYERS
(position, seasons with team)

Sammy Baugh (QB/DB/P, 1937–52)
Larry Brown (RB, 1969–76)
Darrell Green (CB, 1983–2002)
Russ Grimm (G, 1981–91)
Joe Jacoby (OT/G, 1981–93)
Sonny Jurgensen (QB, 1964–74)
Billy Kilmer (QB, 1971–78)
Bobby Mitchell (RB/WR, 1962–68)
Art Monk (WR, 1980–93)
Santana Moss (WR, 2005–14)
John Riggins (RB, 1976–79, 1981–85)
Mark Rypien (QB, 1988–93)
Chris Samuels (OT, 2000–09)
Charley Taylor (RB/WR, 1964–75, 1977)
Joe Theismann (QB, 1974–85)
Doug Williams (QB, 1986–89)
Trent Williams (T, 2010–)

HOME FIELDS

FedEx Field (1997–)
RFK Stadium (1961–96)
  Also known as DC Stadium
Griffith Stadium (1937–60)
Fenway Park (1932–36)

*All statistics through 2018 season

QUOTES AND ANECDOTES

The result of every United States presidential election from 1936 through 2000 followed the outcome of the most recent Redskins home game. Every time the Redskins won, the incumbent party (the party that was already in office) won the election. When the Redskins lost, the incumbent party lost. That changed in 2004, when the Redskins lost to the Green Bay Packers on October 31. Two days later, George W. Bush, the incumbent Republican Party candidate, was reelected.

RFK Stadium, where the Redskins played from 1961 to 1996, was known as one of the most intimidating places for opponents to visit. Although it seated fewer than 60,000 fans, they were close to the field and very loud.

"[Joe] Gibbs would go out, year after year, and work 16 or more hours a day, seven days a week from July through January and sleep on his office cot four nights a week. The purpose: winning football games for the Redskins and being a big success himself."

—Washington Post *columnist Thomas Boswell*

The rivalry between the Redskins and the Dallas Cowboys is one of the most intense in the NFL. "There are three great things in life: winning the lottery, having a baby, and beating the Cowboys this badly," Redskins guard Mark May said after Washington ripped Dallas 41–14 in 1986.

GLOSSARY

All-Pro
An award given to the top players at their positions regardless of their conference. It is a high honor as there are fewer spots on the All-Pro team than on the Pro Bowl teams.

berth
A place, spot, or position, such as in the NFL playoffs.

churning
Moving with vigor and purpose.

commissioner
The chief executive of a sports league.

contract
An agreement to play for a certain team.

dynasty
A team that has an extended period of success, usually winning multiple championships in the process.

general manager
A team employee responsible for negotiating contracts with that team's players.

integrated
Including people of all races.

postseason
Another word for playoffs; the time after the end of the regular season when teams play to determine a champion.

strike
A labor protest that involves refusing to work until certain demands are met.

wild card
A team that makes the playoffs even though it did not win its division.

MORE INFORMATION

BOOKS

Smolka, Bo. *Washington Redskins*. Minneapolis, MN: Abdo Publishing, 2017.

Temple, Ramey. *Washington Redskins*. New York, NY: AV2 by Weigl, 2015.

Zappa, Marcia. *Washington Redskins*. Minneapolis, MN: Abdo Publishing, 2015.

ONLINE RESOURCES

Booklinks
NONFICTION NETWORK
FREE! ONLINE NONFICTION RESOURCES

To learn more about the Washington Redskins, visit **abdobooklinks.com** or scan this QR code. These links are routinely monitored and updated to provide the most current information available.

PLACE TO VISIT

Bon Secours Washington Redskins Training Center
2401 W Leigh St.
Richmond, VA 23220
804–325–8801
redskinsrva.bonsecours.com

This is where Washington holds its training camp prior to each season. Fans are able to watch practice for free and get autographs when the team is done for the day.

INDEX

ABOUT THE AUTHOR

Tony Hunter is a writer from Castle Rock, Colorado. This is his first children's book series. He lives with his daughter and his trusty Rottweiler, Dan.